CATS' TALES
FROM
Shakespeare

Thorsons
An Imprint of HarperCollins Publishers
77-85 Fulham Palace Road,
Hammersmith, London W6 8JB

The Thorsons website address is: www.thorsons.com

First published in Great Britain by Thorsons 2002

10 9 8 7 6 5 4 3 2 1

Illustrations and introductory text © Margaret Woodhouse 2002

Margaret Woodhouse asserts the moral right to be
identified as the author of this work

A catalogue record of this book is available from the British Library

ISBN 0-00-714603-5

Printed and bound in China

Cats' Tales
FROM
Shakespeare

Margaret Woodhouse

Thorsons

4

Shakespeare understood pussycats. His plays are full of descriptive reference to the feline character. He knew how to mould and stroke a literary picture of the mog we all love to have purring amongst us: the brooding hunter; the fixated distaste of things canine; an exquisite relationship with the moon.

Reproduced here are some of his best known transmogrifications, together with some less well-known Shakespearean gems. The illustrations are superb examples of Elizabethan period portraiture.

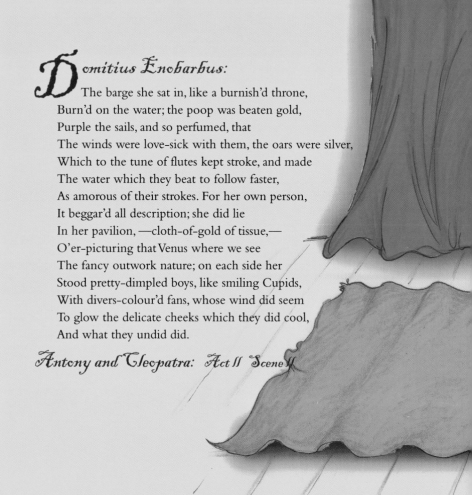

Domitius Enobarbus:

The barge she sat in, like a burnish'd throne,
Burn'd on the water; the poop was beaten gold,
Purple the sails, and so perfumed, that
The winds were love-sick with them, the oars were silver,
Which to the tune of flutes kept stroke, and made
The water which they beat to follow faster,
As amorous of their strokes. For her own person,
It beggar'd all description; she did lie
In her pavilion, —cloth-of-gold of tissue,—
O'er-picturing that Venus where we see
The fancy outwork nature; on each side her
Stood pretty-dimpled boys, like smiling Cupids,
With divers-colour'd fans, whose wind did seem
To glow the delicate cheeks which they did cool,
And what they undid did.

Antony and Cleopatra: Act II Scene II

Duke Orsino:

If music be the food of love, play on;
Give me excess of it, that, surfeiting,
The appetite may sicken, and so die.
That strain again! it had a dying fall:
O! it came o'er my ear like the sweet sound
That breathes upon a bank of violets,
Stealing and giving odour. Enough! no more:
'Tis not so sweet now as it was before.
O spirit of love! how quick and fresh art thou,
That, notwithstanding thy capacity
Receiveth as the sea, nought enters there,
Of what validity and pitch soe'er,
But falls into abatement and low price,
Even in a minute: so full of shapes is fancy,
That it alone is high fantastical.

Twelfth Night: Act 1 Scene 1

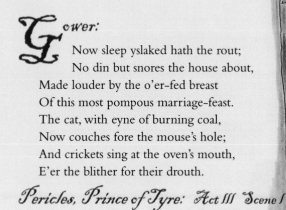

Gower:

Now sleep yslaked hath the rout;
No din but snores the house about,
Made louder by the o'er-fed breast
Of this most pompous marriage-feast.
The cat, with eyne of burning coal,
Now couches fore the mouse's hole;
And crickets sing at the oven's mouth,
E'er the blither for their drouth.

Pericles, Prince of Tyre: Act III Scene 1

Hamlet:

Alas! poor Yorick. I knew him, Horatio; a fellow of infinite jest, of most excellent fancy; he hath borne me on his back a thousand times; and now, how abhorred in my imagination it is! my gorge rises at it. Here hung those lips that I have kissed I know not how oft. Where be your gibes now? your gambols? your songs? your flashes of merriment, that were wont to set the table on a roar? Not one now, to mock your own grinning? quite chapfallen? Now get you to my lady's chamber, and tell her, let her paint an inch thick, to this favour she must come; make her laugh at that.

Hamlet, Prince of Denmark: Act V Scene I

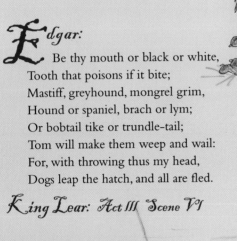

Edgar:

Be thy mouth or black or white,
Tooth that poisons if it bite;
Mastiff, greyhound, mongrel grim,
Hound or spaniel, brach or lym;
Or bobtail tike or trundle-tail;
Tom will make them weep and wail:
For, with throwing thus my head,
Dogs leap the hatch, and all are fled.

King Lear: Act III Scene VI

Dull:

    If a talent be a claw, look how he claws him with a talent.

Love's Labour's Lost: Act IV Scene II

Clarence:

    With that, methought, a legion of foul fiends
Environ'd me, and howled in mine ears
Such hideous cries, that, with the very noise
I trembling wak'd, and, for a season after
Could not believe but that I was in hell;

Richard III: Act I Scene IV

Richard, Duke of Gloucester:

Now is the winter of our discontent
Made glorious summer by this sun of York;
And all the clouds that lour'd upon our house
In the deep bosom of the ocean buried.
Now are our brows bound with victorious wreaths;
Our bruised arms hung up for monuments;
Our stern alarums changed to merry meetings;
Our dreadful marches to delightful measures.
Grim-visag'd war hath smooth'd his wrinkled front;
And now, —instead of mounting barbed steeds,
To fright the souls of fearful adversaries,—
He capers nimbly in a lady's chamber
To the lascivious pleasing of a lute.
But I, that am not shap'd for sportive tricks,
Nor made to court an amorous looking-glass;
I, that am rudely stamp'd, and want love's majesty
To strut before a wanton ambling nymph;
I, that am curtail'd of this fair proportion,
Cheated of feature by dissembling nature,
Deform'd, unfinish'd, sent before my time
Into this breathing world, scarce half made up,
And that so lamely and unfashionable
That dogs bark at me as I halt by them;

Richard III: Act I Scene I

Clifford:

To whom do lions cast their gentle looks?
Not to the beast that would usurp their den.

Henry VI Part 3: Act II Scene II

Henry V:

Once more unto the breach, dear friends, once more;
Or close the wall up with our English dead!
In peace there's nothing so becomes a man
As modest stillness and humility:
But when the blast of war blows in our ears,
Then imitate the action of the tiger;
Stiffen the sinews, summon up the blood,
Disguise fair nature with hard-favour'd rage;
Then lend the eye a terrible aspect;
Let pry through the portage of the head
Like the brass cannon; let the brow o'erwhelm it
As fearfully as doth a galled rock
O'erhang and jutty his confounded base,
Swill'd with the wild and wasteful ocean.
Now set the teeth and stretch the nostril wide,
Hold hard the breath, and bend up every spirit
To his full height!

Henry V: Act III Scene I

Lysander:

Hang off, thou cat, thou burr! vile thing, let loose,
Or I will shake thee from me like a serpent.

A Midsummer Night's Dream: Act III Scene II

Hamlet:

What is the reason that you use me thus?
I lov'd you ever: but it is no matter;
Let Hercules himself do what he may,
The cat will mew and dog will have his day.

Hamlet, Prince of Denmark: Act V Scene 1

Witches:
Double, double toil and trouble;
Fire burn and cauldron bubble.

Second Witch:
Fillet of a fenny snake,
In the cauldron boil and bake;
Eye of newt, and toe of frog,
Wool of bat, and tongue of dog,
Adder's fork, and blind-worm's sting,
Lizard's leg and howlet's wing,
For a charm of powerful trouble,
Like a hell-broth boil and bubble.

Macbeth: Act IV Scene I

M *ercutio:*

More than prince of cats, I can tell you.
O! he is the courageous captain of compliments.
He fights as you sing prick-song, keeps time,
distance, and proportion; rests me his minum rest,
one, two, and the third in your bosom; the very
butcher of a silk button, a duellist, a duellist; a
gentleman of the very first house, of the first and
second cause. Ah! the immortal passado! the punto
reverso! the hay!

Romeo and Juliet: Act II Scene IV

Queen Margaret:

  O Buckingham! take heed of yonder dog:
  Look, when he fawns, he bites; and when he bites
His venom tooth will rankle to the death:
Have not to do with him, beware of him;
Sin, death and hell have set their marks on him,
And all their ministers attend on him.

Richard III: Act I Scene III

Amiens:

Under the greenwood tree
Who loves to lie with me,
And turn his merry note
Unto the sweet bird's throat,
Come hither, come hither, come hither:
Here shall he see
No enemy
But winter and rough weather.

As You Like It: Act II Scene V

Theseus:

    Question your desires;
    Know of your youth, examine well your blood,
    Whether, if you yield not to your father's choice,
    You can endure the livery of a nun,
    For aye to be in shady cloister mew'd,
    To live a barren sister all your life,
    Chanting faint hymns to the cold fruitless moon.

A Midsummer Night's Dream: Act I Scene I

Second Page:

It was a lover and his lass,
  With a hey, and a ho, and a hey nonino,
That o'er the green corn-field did pass,
  In the spring time, the only pretty ring time,
When birds do sing, hey ding a ding, ding;
Sweet lovers love the spring.

Between the acres of the rye,
  With a hey, and a ho, and a hey nonino,
These pretty country folks would lie,
  In the spring time, the only pretty ring time,
When birds do sing, hey ding a ding, ding;
Sweet lovers love the spring.

As You Like It: Act V Scene III

Lorenzo:

The moon shines bright: in such a night as this,
When the sweet wind did gently kiss the trees
And they did make no noise, in such a night
Troilus methinks mounted the Troyan walls,
And sigh'd his soul toward the Grecian tents,
Where Cressid lay that night.

The Merchant of Venice: Act V Scene 1

King Henry IV:

O sleep! O gentle sleep!
Nature's soft nurse;

Henry IV Part 2: Act III Scene I

𝓛ady 𝓜acbeth:

Out, damned spot! out, I say!

𝓜acbeth: 𝓐ct V 𝓢cene 1

Caesar:

    Let me have men about me that are fat;
Sleek-headed men and such as sleep o' nights.
Yond Cassius has a lean and hungry look;
He thinks too much: such men are dangerous.

Julius Caesar: Act I Scene II

Edgar:

Poor Tom; that eats the swimming frog;
the toad, the tadpole, the wall-newt, and the
water; that in the fury of his heart, when
the foul fiend rages, eats cow-dung for
sallets; swallows the old rat and the ditch-
dog; drinks the green mantle of the
standing pool; who is whipped from tithing
to tithing, and stock-punished, and
imprisoned; who hath had three suits to his
back, six shirts to his body, horse to ride,
and weapon to wear;
But mice and rats and such small deer
Have been Tom's food for seven long year.

King Lear: Act III Scene IV

44

Macbeth:

Is this a dagger which I see before me,
The handle toward my hand? Come, let me clutch thee:
I have thee not, and yet I see thee still.
Art thou not, fatal vision, sensible
To feeling as to sight? or art thou but
A dagger of the mind, a false creation,
Proceeding from the heat-oppressed brain?
I see thee yet, in form as palpable
As this which now I draw.
Thou marshall'st me the way that I was going;
And such an instrument I was to use.
Mine eyes are made the fools o' the other senses,
Or else worth all the rest: I see thee still;
And on thy blade and dudgeon gouts of blood,
Which was not so before. There's no such thing:
It is the bloody business which informs
Thus to mine eyes. Now o'er the one halfworld
Nature seems dead, and wicked dreams abuse
The curtain'd sleep; witchcraft celebrates
Pale Hecate's offerings; and wither'd murder,
Alarum'd by his sentinel, the wolf,
Whose howl's his watch, thus with his stealthy pace.
With Tarquin's ravishing strides, toward his design
Moves like a ghost. Thou sure and firm-set earth,
Hear not my steps, which way they walk, for fear
Thy very stones prate of my whereabout,
And take the present horror from the time,
Which now suits with it. Whiles I threat he lives:
Words to the heat of deeds too cold breath gives.
I go, and it is done; the bell invites me.
Hear it not, Duncan; for it is a knell
That summons thee to heaven or to hell.

Macbeth: Act II Scene I

Menenius:

Thou rascal, that art worst in blood to run,
Lead'st first to win some vantage.
But make you ready your stiff bats and clubs:
Rome and her rats are at the point of battle;

Coriolanus: Act 1 Scene 1

Portia:

The quality of mercy is not strain'd,
It droppeth as the gentle rain from heaven
Upon the place beneath: it is twice bless'd;
It blesseth him that gives and him that takes:
'Tis mightiest in the mightiest; it becomes
The throned monarch better than his crown;
His sceptre shows the force of temporal power,
The attribute to awe and majesty,
Wherein doth sit the dread and fear of kings;
But mercy is above this sceptred sway,
It is enthroned in the hearts of kings,
It is an attribute to God himself,
And earthly power doth then show likest God's
When mercy seasons justice.

The Merchant of Venice: Act IV Scene I

Petruchio:

Come, Kate, and wash, and welcome heartily.

The Taming of the Shrew: Act IV Scene I

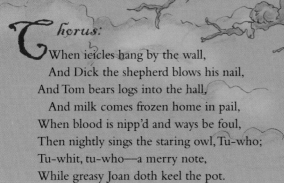

Chorus:

When icicles hang by the wall,
    And Dick the shepherd blows his nail,
And Tom bears logs into the hall,
    And milk comes frozen home in pail,
When blood is nipp'd and ways be foul,
Then nightly sings the staring owl, Tu-who;
Tu-whit, tu-who—a merry note,
While greasy Joan doth keel the pot.

When all aloud the wind doth blow,
    And coughing drowns the parson's saw,
And birds sit brooding in the snow,
    And Marian's nose looks red and raw,
When roasted crabs hiss in the bowl,
Then nightly sings the staring owl, Tu-who;
Tu-whit, tu-who—a merry note,
While greasy Joan doth keel the pot.

Love's Labour's Lost: Act V Scene II

Autolycus:

The lark, that tirra-lirra chants,
With, heigh! with, heigh! the thrush and the jay,
Are summer songs for me and my aunts,
While we lie tumbling in the hay.

The Winter's Tale: Act IV Scene II

Oberon:

Ill met by moonlight, proud Titania

A Midsummer Night's Dream: Act II Scene 1

Juliet:

O Romeo, Romeo! wherefore art thou Romeo?

Romeo and Juliet: Act II Scene II

Puck

Now the hungry lion roars,
  And the wolf behowls the moon;
Whilst the heavy ploughman snores,
  All with weary task fordone.
Now the wasted brands do glow,
  Whilst the screech-owl, screeching loud,
Puts the wretch that lies in woe
  In remembrance of a shroud.
Now it is the time of night
  That the graves all gaping wide,
Every one lets forth his sprite,
  In the church-way paths to glide:
And we fairies, that do run
  By the triple Hecate's team,
From the presence of the sun,
  Following darkness like a dream,
Now are frolic: not a mouse
Shall disturb this hallow'd house:
I am sent with broom before,
To sweep the dust behind the door.

A Midsummer Night's Dream: Act V Scene I

Sampson:

A dog of the house of Montague moves me.

Romeo and Juliet: Act 1 Scene 1